THE SEVENTH REQUEST

THE SEVENTH REQUEST

Change the Way You Think About Prayer

ANNA SCATES

Insignis Interactive
Satsuma, AL

The Seventh Request
Copyright © 2017 by Anna Scates, 7yearadventure.com

All rights reserved. No portion of this book may be reproduced, stored in a retrieval system, or transmitted in any form or by any means—electronic, mechanical, photocopy, recording, scanning, or other—except for brief quotations in critical reviews or articles, without the prior written permission of the publisher.

Scripture quotations, unless otherwise noted, are taken from the Holy Bible, New Living Translation, copyright ©1996, 2004, 2007, by Tyndale House Foundation. Used by permission of Tyndale House Publishers, Inc., Carol Stream, Illinois 60188. All rights reserved.

ISBN-13: 978-1-946730-01-5
ISBN-10: 1-946730-01-7

Edited by Jacquelyn McCray
Cover Photo by Anna Scates
Author Photo by Andrea Scates
Layout & Cover Design by James Woosley, FreeAgentPress.com

Published by Insignis Interactive
InsignisInteractive.com
Satsuma, Alabama 36572
VID: 20170924

This book is dedicated to my wonderful family

To my husband, Don, for his hard work and tireless devotion to our family, and for always loving me and supporting me no matter how many hair-brained ideas I have.

To my daughter, Jacquelyn, whose proofreading and editing skills are unsurpassed, and who, in addition to being my daughter, has also masterfully filled the precious roles of sister, best friend, and chief confidant.

To my son, Graham, whose sunny disposition and eternal optimism serve as encouragement and inspiration to me whenever I need it, and who has the unique ability to brighten my day merely with the sweet sound of his voice.

To my mother, Nell, and my father, Donald, who taught me faith in God and a love for the Bible at a young age, and who taught me that I could accomplish whatever I set my mind to do.

Finally to my daughter, Andrea, without whom this book would not exist, who has elevated the concept of determination to a new level, and whose presence in this world was most certainly meant to be.

Contents

Introduction ix

Chapter 1: Wanting More 1

Chapter 2: My Plan vs. God's Plan 7

Chapter 3: No Surprises, Please 11

Chapter 4: Blindsided (Surprise!)................................. 17

Chapter 5: Learning the True Power of Prayer 23

Chapter 6: Growing the Faith 31

Chapter 7: Praying Specifically 43

Chapter 8: God Answers Prayer
(and He Drives a Pickup Truck) 51

Chapter 9: Let It Go 61

Chapter 10: Ecstasy & Agony 65

Chapter 11: A Bigger Fig Tree 71

Chapter 12: Specific Prayer—Round 2 83

Chapter 13: The Seventh Request Fulfilled 93

Chapter 14: The Happy Ending 97

Notes 99

About the Cover 117

About the Author 119

Introduction

It was difficult for me to get down to business and finally write this book. I realized many years ago that I wanted to share with others what I had learned about improving my prayer life. After the experiences that taught me so much about the importance of praying specifically for our needs, I thought I should begin to record what had happened, but I could not get the words written down. Something held me back.

As time progressed, and more events took place, I realized why I was being held back. The reason I could not write my story was because it had not all happened yet. There were still so many more events to transpire to make the story complete. And I had so much more to learn.

This completed story is what's presented here now. The goal is for my journey of growth in my prayer life to be colorfully illustrated by the account of our unusual circumstances, and punctuated by the lessons I took with me from the scriptures along the way.

My fondest prayer is that God will use my words to bless your life in some mighty way. May I decrease so He might increase.

1

Wanting More

Have you ever known a person who always wants to strive for more, even when it seems she already has all she could possibly need or want? I certainly am that person, and if you are like that, too, then we have a lot in common. We can't help it. It's the way we're wired.

I had more than enough blessings to make me happy. I had a fantastic husband, two adorable healthy children, a lovely home, and wonderful friends and family. Enviable by any standard. So how could I possibly want something else? It's a normal course we human beings take. We have what we want, so what is our natural reaction? We want more.

What else could I have wanted, though?

The answer—another baby, of course.

There was something about a third child that seemed as though it would make our family complete. We already had a girl and a boy, two and a half years apart. Perfect, right? But still something inside me wanted that third baby. I had the feeling of not being finished, a feeling there was still one more person who was meant to be.

> "I had the feeling of not being finished, a feeling there was still one more person who was meant to be."

Since I had been an only child, I did not want just one child. I wanted several children who would grow up together so they could have that close family element throughout their lives into adulthood. There would be no first cousins for them on either side of the family, and therefore limited extended family in the future. My kids would only have each other and the families they would create.

I had it all planned out. Lots of people do that, and that's a good thing. They plan what they want their lives to look like. I did that, too. My childbearing would consist of my first baby being born when I was 27. I got that one in under the wire, because I miscarried my first pregnancy. That baby was due on July 14, 1992, but it was not meant to be. Instead, almost one year to the day after I miscarried, we were blessed with Jacquelyn in December of 1992.

I planned to have my next child at age 30. Right on schedule and as planned, Graham was born in July of 1995. Great! I am right on track. Only one more, to be born when

I was 33. That way, I would be finished before age 35, when certain risk factors kicked in.

Yep, I had it all planned out. But God had something different in mind. He always does.

> "God had something different in mind. He always does."

In 1997, my husband and I lived in a beautiful home in Waverly, Tennessee surrounded in the community by some of the most wonderful people I have ever known. We had our four-year-old daughter and our two-year-old son. They were beautiful, and I was happy with our family and our life together. Everything seemed to fit just right. We had the perfect number of seats in the vehicle, and the right number of bedrooms in the house. Even our breakfast table was the right size. A family of four is what our whole society seems to be designed for.

I almost felt guilty for wanting more than I already had. Aren't we supposed to be satisfied and content with our blessings? Still, I felt the need for that third baby nagging away inside of me. I couldn't shake it. It was on my mind constantly.

Food for Thought

During that time, I decided to look up verses in the Bible that had to do with contentment, verses that dealt with the concept of wanting more.

When I did this, most of what I read pertained to financial wealth and greed. That's fine, but what about the factor of contentment that has nothing to do with money?

I was not dissatisfied with our financial state. I suppose everyone wants a bigger bank account, but when I say I wanted more, money was not my focus. It was about having another baby, increasing our family.

> *"...when I say I wanted more, money was not my focus."*

So I began to look at examples of women in the Bible who were blessed in multiple ways, but wanted children they could not have. Those examples seemed to fit my mindset better than the verses geared towards helping us overcome our greed.

Here are some of the women who inspired me:

- **Sarah** – Sarah was blessed throughout her life and into her old age with a wealthy and powerful husband, Abraham. But the main thing that had been missing from her life was a child.
- **Rachel** – The second, but preferred, wife of Jacob also had a husband who was wealthy and powerful,

and he loved her most of all his wives. She had everything she could have desired—but it wasn't enough. She wanted a baby more than anything, and nothing else would satisfy her.

- **Leah** – The first wife of Jacob had already been blessed with four children, but she was unhappy because she knew her husband did not love her, and she fought continuously with her sister, Rachel. Leah prayed for more children, and God heard and granted her petitions.

- **Hannah** – The eventual mother of Samuel, once again, was blessed with material possessions and a husband who loved her more than his other wife and the rest of his family. But nothing comforted her. She wept for a baby.

- **Elizabeth** – The woman who gave birth to John the Baptist, the one who paved the way for the Lord Jesus, was yet another example of an old woman who had been blessed throughout her life with wealth and prestige, and a devoted husband, Zechariah, who was a Jewish priest. But her desire for a child overshadowed the other blessings in her life.

In each of these examples, the Lord never condemned the women or seemed to be displeased with them for wanting more, even though some of their husbands weighed in a bit in that direction. Perhaps it's because it was not material possessions they craved, but the privilege and honor of motherhood they desired most. Eventually, God blessed each of them with the deepest desires of their hearts.

> *"...the Lord never condemned the women or seemed to be displeased with them for wanting more..."*

But what if He chooses not to do that? Sometimes God says "Yes" to our requests, but sometimes He answers "No." It is so difficult for us to be patient and wait on God's answers, especially for those of us who need to plan out the fine details of our lives.

2

My Plan vs. God's Plan

I HAVE ALWAYS BEEN A firm believer in the benefits of nursing. I nursed my babies until it became evident that it was time to stop, about 15 months for each of the first two. After I stopped nursing my son, I waited patiently for things to return to normal so I would be able to get pregnant again. But things did not return to normal.

Long after Graham stopped nursing, I was still producing milk. That was strange, and warranted visits to doctors to figure out what was going on. I had to search for a new doctor other than the one who delivered my first two babies because we had moved about two hours away.

The first doctor I visited listened hurriedly to the description of my symptoms. He made an on-the-spot diagnosis that I had a "cluster of cells," as he put it, on my pituitary gland causing me to have this problem. He performed no further tests. He prescribed some medication and told me to come back in six weeks or sooner if I became pregnant.

I did, indeed, become pregnant. Great! And right on schedule. My plans were about to be derailed if I didn't get pregnant soon.

My plans.

> "My plans were about to be derailed if I didn't get pregnant soon."

I contacted that same doctor's office to make an appointment since I did confirm that I was pregnant, but they were very difficult to work with and even rude. It was clear that I needed to find another doctor's office immediately.

After locating a very good doctor in Nashville, Tennessee, someone whom my friends had highly recommended, I visited her office and she also confirmed that I was pregnant. She was, however, shocked at the medication the other doctor had prescribed. She wondered why he did not do any further testing if he felt those meds were warranted. She ordered me to stop taking them immediately since I had become pregnant.

I made my first prenatal exam appointment with this new doctor, and we were off and running. My due date was April 15, 1998. Yay! A spring baby. Wonderful, and I would be 33 the January before that, so everything was perfect. Right on schedule.

Just like I had planned.

Food for Thought

Isn't it funny how God sometimes has other plans that don't even resemble ours? At the time when we're experiencing the tough stuff, we can't really see God working. We get so caught up in our own plans, wishes, desires, obstacles, and problems that we lose sight of the bigger picture. That's why we have to trust Him.

> "At the time when we're experiencing the tough stuff, we can't really see God working."

God allows us to experience those trials so our faith in Him will grow and mature, and His power will be evident. He also uses us to bless other people during our troubled times.

The Apostle Paul struggled with wanting God to take away a problem he was having, and waiting on God to answer the request. God's response to him is found in this passage of scripture:

2 Corinthians 12:9 (NLT)

But he said to me, "My Grace is sufficient for you, for my power is made perfect in weakness."

Wow! Through my weakness, His strength is evident; therefore, my plans and desires have to take a backseat to His perfect will.

But sometimes finding that will isn't so easy.

3

No Surprises, Please

My mother and dad came to visit us shortly after that last doctor's visit, and I shared with them the wonderful news about our pregnancy. We were all thrilled, and thus began the process of planning for baby number three.

During that visit, we went out in town for lunch. Afterwards, we stopped at a local gift shop owned by my friend, Rita, to look around at the things she had on sale. Lots of people in town were doing the same thing, including Lori, one of my very good friends. She was a devout Christian, a true prayer warrior, and one of the godliest women I have ever known.

At this time, no one else knew our little secret. It was so early, we only had time to make the announcement to my parents. Also, I liked to wait a little while before telling others about our pending bundles of joy. Based on the experience with my first pregnancy and miscarriage, it was easier if I didn't have to un-tell people our news later just in case something bad were to happen.

I went over to Lori and hugged her. She hugged me back, and held onto me a little bit long. She then whispered in my ear, "I don't want to alarm you, but God laid it on my heart this morning during my devotional time that you are going to need prayer."

> "...God laid it on my heart this morning ... that you are going to need prayer."

She pulled back and we looked at each other for another moment. She apologized and said she didn't want to upset me, and obviously she didn't know why, but she felt God was urging her to tell me that. I thanked her and told her it was okay, and that I was glad she had told me.

At that moment, I knew.

In my heart of hearts and in the core of my being, I knew exactly what God was preparing me for. I was going to lose this baby.

I walked away from the store, got into my van with my parents and my two little kids, and drove back home. The whole way I pondered what Lori had told me.

I did not mention anything about the incident to anyone else. I couldn't bring myself to believe it or dwell on it anymore, even though I knew why God had spoken to Lori. I certainly couldn't voice it. That would sound crazy, nuts. I tried to dismiss it from my mind, but without success.

> "In my heart of hearts and in the core of my being, I knew exactly what God was preparing me for."

How could this be? He knew what my plans were. How could God allow this to happen? But it hadn't happened. No. I was just letting my imagination run away with me. Or was I?

I used to think I liked surprises, but the more I live, the more I realize that I am not so fond of them, unless they involve flowers or chocolate. God knows this about me, of course, and through Lori, He sent me the warning He knew I would need.

A few days later, on a Saturday in late August, I did indeed lose that baby. My husband had gone to his parents' farm to help out that particular day, so it was just me at home with my two little ones. The words of my friend Lori echoed in my ears. "You're going to need prayer." How true that was.

After it was over, I cried as I held onto my babies. Of course I cried, and my little ones had no idea why Mommy was sad.

> "After it was over, I cried as I held onto my babies."

I contacted my new doctor the following Monday, and explained to her what had happened. She brought me in to do an exam, and we talked. I told her about all the strange things that had been happening, such as the extended lactation, and all the other problems I was having that were seemingly unrelated: the extreme fatigue, the debilitating headaches, the weird and almost non-existent menstrual cycles before getting pregnant while on the medication, among other factors.

Based on all the information I shared with her that day, she decided to refer me to an endocrinologist.

Food for Thought

What does the Bible say about handling heartbreak?

Few people in the Bible are more familiar with heartbreak, fear, and suffering than David. His words of comfort are found in the Psalms, particularly **Psalm 34:18**, where he says that God is close by to provide comfort when people are brokenhearted, or **Psalm 71:20**, where he states that God will bring us back from the depths of the earth and give us new life.

> **Psalm 34:18 (NLT)**
>
> The Lord is close to the brokenhearted; he rescues those whose spirits are crushed.

> **Psalm 71:20 (NLT)**
>
> You have allowed me to suffer much hardship, but you will restore me to life again and lift me up from the depths of the earth.

Don't give up hope, even when things seem sad and hopeless. True to His word, God carries us through. Sometimes, we might have to wait on Him, but hang on. It is worth it.

4

Blindsided (Surprise!)

Dr. Andrea Hays was very young, as doctors go, and fresh out of residency, just starting her endocrinology practice. She was only a few months older than I was—age 32. She brought me into her office and we sat and talked for a long time. I told her everything as she listened intently and made lots of notes. I truly felt like she cared about getting to the root of my problem, and I appreciated her kind attention.

After listening to all my ramblings, and trying skillfully to piece it all together, Dr. Hays decided I needed to have an MRI. Having never had anything like that before, I was clueless about what I was in for.

My dear friend, Lori, kept Jacquelyn and Graham for me while I made the trip to Nashville alone to have this test done. I was very apprehensive about it, and concerned about what they might find, especially because she chose to have the MRI done on my head. I didn't understand how that would tie in with all my symptoms.

> "I was very apprehensive …, and concerned about what they might find…"

The MRI alone took at least an hour, in addition to all the preparation and wait time associated with such an appointment. Since I am claustrophobic, having to keep my head very still inside that loud, cramped, enclosed tunnel was something I needed God's help to endure.

All of that took place on Monday afternoon, October 13, 1997.

I was getting ready to go to my weekly Bible study group meeting on the following Tuesday morning, October 14. As I was drying and styling my hair, the phone rang. It was Dr. Hays.

She informed me that the radiologist called her about my MRI results because he saw something that called for immediate attention. She went on to state that she did not like to give news like this over the phone, but she was going out of town that morning and would be out of the office for the rest of the week. She felt I should know before she left.

"That's fine. Go ahead and tell me. I want to know now," I said. I was bracing myself, trying to control the butterflies in my stomach. I couldn't imagine what she was going to say.

"You have a tumor," she began with a rather guarded tone. "It's roughly the size of a Ping-Pong ball, and it's under your brain, growing on your pituitary gland. Again I am so sorry for having to tell you this on the phone."

I was speechless for a few moments.

What? A tumor? Under my brain? That couldn't be right. On the pituitary gland? What does that even do? My mind was reeling with questions as I stood in silence, trying to take in what I had heard. It felt like I was having some bizarre, out-of-body experience.

> "It felt like I was having some bizarre, out-of-body experience."

I had not even considered the possibility of a brain tumor, or a pituitary tumor, or whatever it was. And not being terribly familiar with the endocrine system, I was not even sure where or what the pituitary gland was, let alone why it was important. And how could a tumor there be the root of all the issues I'd been having?

Dr. Hays went on to explain what the radiologist had seen, and attempted to answer some of my many questions.

The pituitary gland sits right at the base of the brain, just about in the center of a person's head. It is straight behind the bridge of the nose, and it governs nearly every hormone secretion in the body. This tumor was sitting right on top of the gland and apparently growing up under my brain and into my optic nerve chiasm, stretching it, and endangering my eyesight. That explained the frequent, excruciating headaches.

To make matters worse, it was secreting a large amount of growth hormone into my system, causing my bones, joints, hands, and feet to grow, a condition known as acromegaly. That explained a lot more, like why my ring size and shoe size kept increasing.

I was finally able to connect the dots between all those odd symptoms and conclude that they were very related. Dr. Hays was brilliant for figuring all that out.

> *"I was finally able to connect the dots between all those odd symptoms…"*

The good news was that tumors of this sort are historically non-malignant, so my cancer risk was not terribly high, although it was possible. Still, all things considered, that was a positive note. I felt there were already enough other things to worry about.

When I hung up the phone with Dr. Hays, it took a few minutes for all of that to finally sink in.

A brain tumor. I did not see that one coming.

Food for Thought

We've all been blindsided.

Often people experience things that are unexpected at best. Life is full of those little gems that crop up and pop up and sometimes trip us up. They appear out of nowhere, and can take our lives by storm.

What does God tell us in His word about our best-laid plans, and the ability to adapt to the unexpected things that may happen to us?

The book of James provides some insight.

> **James 4:13-16 (NLT)**
>
> ¹³Look here, you who say, "Today or tomorrow we are going to a certain town and will stay there a year. We will do business there, and make a profit." ¹⁴How do you know what your life will be like tomorrow? Your life is like the morning fog—it's here a little while, then it's gone. ¹⁵What you ought to say is, "If the Lord wants us to, we will live and do this or that." ¹⁶Otherwise you are boasting about your own plans, and all such boasting is evil.

I'll be honest. It's difficult for me sometimes to wrap my mind around the fact that planning something can be considered evil in God's eyes, but according to this passage, it is.

> *"It's difficult for me ... to wrap my mind around the fact that planning something can be considered evil in God's eyes..."*

Don't misunderstand. God does expect us to plan and be responsible, as Solomon states in **Proverbs 6:6-8**, where he uses the industrious little ant as an example to be emulated.

BUT. When our plans begin to overshadow God's, then sometimes those unexpected obstacles are necessary to keep us on His track.

5

LEARNING THE
TRUE POWER OF PRAYER

I **ALWAYS HAD A FEAR** of dying and leaving my children. I had no siblings of my own, and my husband's brothers were unmarried and living in other cities. My parents also lived several hours away, and my husband's job was highly demanding. The slightly nagging question, which was ordinarily in the background of my mind, began to loom before me now: Who would take care of my babies if something happened to me? The thought terrified me.

All I could think about after hearing news like I had just heard was what might happen.

What would we do? What if it's cancerous? What if I die? How can Jacquelyn and Graham grow up without their mama? How can I miss all those wonderful moments and milestones that all mothers dream of experiencing?

> "Who would take care of my babies if something happened to me?"

The sweet hugs and kisses. The musical sound of their voices. The first days of school. The games, competitions, and awards. The accomplishments. The graduations. The weddings.

It was more than I could stand.

I pulled them close to me and sank down to the floor of my daughter's bedroom on my knees in front of one of the closets. The scene is permanently etched on the window of my soul. I held them for a long time and just cried. They were so sweet, wondering why Mommy was sad—again.

It was a good thing, and a God thing, that Dr. Hays did not make me drive all the way to Nashville (about 70 miles one way) to give me that news. I would never have made it home. It was a blessing that she had to tell me on the phone. A huge blessing.

After sitting on the floor clutching my four-and-a-half-year-old daughter and two-year-old son, I began to pray. I prayed like I had never prayed before in my life. I prayed with fervent determination. I prayed for strength and healing, and for guidance on what to do next.

Suddenly, I felt a peace wash over me, a feeling that my sweet children were not going to lose their mother before they would even remember who I was or anything about me. I simply could not bear that thought. I asked God what I should do next, and He told me.

> "I prayed like I had never prayed before in my life."

First, call your husband and your parents to tell them what's happening. Then go on over to your Tuesday morning Bible study. You're going to need it.

* * *

Of course I was running late after the eventful morning I'd had. I pulled my car up to the door of the church, and got my children out to take them into the nursery. Even though I had tried to fix my makeup, I knew I looked wretched from crying earlier, because I do *not* cry pretty. As I walked them into the nursery, one of the nursery workers, a sweet, perceptive lady, took one look at me and knew something was very wrong. When she asked what was going on, the floodgates opened.

After I finished my spiel, she looked me squarely in the eye, took my hand and patted it, and said, "Come with me." She led me downstairs to where the Bible study group was meeting. She interrupted the study session and explained to them what I had told her.

As soon as she finished, there was an immediate outpouring of love and support from the group. All of those precious ladies gathered around me, each one laying a hand on my shoulder or back, and they all prayed over me, each one individually uttering her petition to God for my swift and complete healing.

> *"All of those precious ladies gathered around me, each one laying a hand on my shoulder or back, and they all prayed over me..."*

I gained a first-hand appreciation for the true meaning and significance of **James 5:13-16**. This passage talks about going to the church elders and having them lay hands on the sick to heal them. Traditionally, we think of those elders as being men. Let me assure you, I have never felt the presence of God more than when I was with those wonderful ladies in my Bible study group. Church elders are also most certainly the women.

> **James 5:13-16 (NLT)**
>
> [13]Are any of you suffering hardships? You should pray. Are any of you happy? You should sing praises. [14]Are any of you sick? You should call for the elders of the church to come and pray over you, anointing you with oil in the name of the Lord. [15]Such a prayer offered in faith will heal the sick, and the Lord will make you well. And if you have committed any sins, you will be forgiven. [16]The earnest prayer of a righteous person has great power and produces wonderful results.

What an amazing, transforming experience!

I had never felt the power of the Holy Spirit like I did at that moment. I could feel God's comfort, grace, and mercy, and another wave of peace came over me. The next level of peace beyond what I had experienced at home while clutching my babies. The peace that surpasses all understanding. I truly understood what Paul meant when he made that statement in **Philippians 4:7**.

> **Philippians 4:7 (NKJV)**
>
> and the peace of God, which surpasses all understanding, will guard your hearts and minds through Christ Jesus.
>
> *Scripture taken from the New King James Version®. Copyright © 1982 by Thomas Nelson. Used by permission. All rights reserved.*

> *"I could feel God's comfort, grace, and mercy, and another wave of peace came over me."*

I realized God was going to get me through this.

Word about my situation began to spread quickly through the church, and throughout the community. We told our family and friends across the United States, and asked them to pray for healing. We had family stretching North to South, from Connecticut to Florida, and East to West, from North Carolina to California. My cousin and her husband in Hawaii were praying for me, and also some friends who had recently moved to Hong Kong. Even some missionaries to Ethiopia from our church, who were about to go off furlough and return to the field, learned of my situation and began praying for me. I had people praying for me all around the world, not to mention the wonderful prayer warriors right there in my Bible study group.

It was incredible—and humbling.

Food for Thought

Have you ever considered the true power of prayer? The power of being able to communicate directly with God?

Verse 16 of the passage in James cited above states that the earnest prayer of a righteous person has great power, and produces wonderful results.

That is a huge revelation, and a huge responsibility.

Many examples exist in the scriptures of people who were setting out to accomplish the will of God, and who prayed earnestly to the Lord for help. Their prayers were answered in a mighty way. Two such examples are Joshua and Elijah:

1. Joshua

When Joshua and the Israelite armies were fighting the battle with the Amorite kings' armies (described in **Joshua 10**), he prayed for more daylight so he could finish what God had commanded him to do. God disrupted His own laws of motion and physics and allowed the earth to pause in its rotation. All because one man, Joshua, prayed.

> **Joshua 10:12-14 (NLT)**
>
> [12]On the day the Lord gave the Israelites victory over the Amorites, Joshua prayed to the Lord in front of all the people of Israel, He said,
>
> "Let the sun stand still over Gibeon, and the moon over the valley of Aijalon."

¹³So the sun stood still and the moon stayed
in place until the nation of Israel had defeated
its enemies.

Is this event not recorded in The Book of
Jashar? The sun stayed in the middle of the
sky, and it did not set as on a normal day.
¹⁴There has never been a day like this one
before or since, when the Lord fought for
Israel that day!

Truly magnificent.

2. Elijah

When Elijah went to King Ahab to warn him of God's wrath over his evil reign of Israel, Elijah prayed for drought. Because of one man's prayer, the heavens closed up for more than three years, and no rain fell on the region.

Right on the heels of our earlier referenced passage from the book of James is this verse:

James 5:17 (NLT)

Elijah was as human as we are, and yet when
he prayed earnestly that no rain would fall,
none fell for three and a half years!

With these examples in mind, think about how much power God endowed His children with when He bestowed the honor and privilege of prayer on us. It is the ability to speak with Him directly. If we effectively tap that great resource of life, God can bless us in ways we never imagined. He can get us through those bumps and obstacles, as well as the nightmares, and He can help us formulate new plans when the old, selfish ones go awry.

> "If we effectively tap that great resource of life, God can bless us in ways we never imagined."

Fortunately, He guides us throughout His word on *how to pray* and *what we should pray for*.

6

GROWING THE FAITH

EVERY DOCTOR'S APPOINTMENT WAS an education. Sometimes we learned things that relieved our fears of the worst, and other times we learned things that greatly added to our concerns.

In addition to seeing Dr. Hays, I went to a neuro-ophthalmologist to have my eyesight checked. He determined that I was, indeed, losing my peripheral vision.

I also went to see a neurosurgeon and an ear-nose-throat surgeon, because they would work together to perform the surgery I needed. They would make an incision inside my mouth, above my top front teeth and go behind my nose, through my sinus cavity to get to the tumor in the center of my head.

It would take the expertise of both doctors to do it successfully. The surgery was scheduled for Monday, November 3, 1997, exactly three weeks after the MRI.

So I used those three weeks to pray and read the Bible and pray some more. It was a time of preparation for me, mentally and spiritually. It's amazing to me to see how God uses situations like this to bring us closer to Him.

> "It's amazing to me to see how God uses situations like this to bring us closer to Him."

Every morning I would scour the scriptures for passages that would help me gain more knowledge from Him about how I should proceed, knowledge directly from Jesus himself on how and why I should have unbridled faith in His ability and His desire to heal me. I started with the seeds of that faith, and day by day they grew and flourished.

I spent a lot of time reading the book of Luke. Since Luke was a physician, and I was having medical issues, this made a lot of sense to me. I enjoyed his sympathetic writing style, and how he seemed almost ahead of his time in his desire to minister to the body, soul, and spirit of his fellow human beings. I particularly loved the fact that Luke so carefully chronicles the thoughts and feelings of Mary, the mother of Jesus, and several other women in his writings.

Coincidentally, we had been doing a study of Luke and Acts in my weekly Bible study group. I actually do not believe it was a coincidence at all. Everything happens for a reason, and I believe God perfectly timed that study for me.

I was particularly drawn to four passages in the Bible that helped me to learn not only how to increase my faith in Jesus' ability and willingness to heal me, but also how to pray specifically for the outcome I desired, and to understand why this was happening to me.

The first passage was **Luke 8:43-48**. This is the account of the woman who had suffered with continuous bleeding. For twelve years she endured this awful condition. She had spent all her money on doctors, but none could provide a cure.

The ramifications of this condition in Jewish culture were significant for this woman. The flow of blood meant she was unclean, according to Levitical law, and this profoundly affected her life. She could not go into the synagogue for worship with her friends and family. She was unable to visit or socialize with anyone. No one could touch her, or even touch any object she came in contact with. She was completely cut off, an outcast of society, and Jesus was her last hope.

> "She was completely cut off, an outcast of society, and Jesus was her last hope."

In this scene, there was a huge crowd, thronging around Jesus and his disciples. People were pressing against Him from all sides, trying to be close to Him. She does her best to fly under the radar, and get as close to Jesus as she possibly can. Just one touch on the hem of his cloak, she thought, and I can be rid of this dreadful plague.

Sure enough, her faith was well placed. After a mere touch of Jesus' garment, she experienced immediate healing. But Jesus, being God in the flesh, knew everything. He knew someone had touched Him, and He knew who she was and why she did it. Yet He asked the question, "Who touched me?"

Terrified of making Him angry, she fell at His feet and told Him and the crowd what she had done and why she had done it. She also told them she had been instantly healed.

Jesus showed compassion to that woman, and told her that her faith had healed her.

Her *faith*.

> "Jesus...told her that her faith had healed her."

Luke 8:43-48 (NLT)

[43] A woman in the crowd had suffered for twelve years with constant bleeding, and she could find no cure. [44] Coming up behind Jesus, she touched the fringe of his robe. Immediately, the bleeding stopped.

[45] "Who touched me?" Jesus asked.

Everyone denied it, and Peter said, "Master, this whole crowd is pressing up against you."

[46] But Jesus said, "Someone deliberately touched me, for I felt healing power go out from me."

[47] When the woman realized that she could not stay hidden, she began to tremble and fell to her knees in front of him. The whole crowd heard her explain why she had touched him and that she had been immediately healed. [48] "Daughter," he said to her, "your faith has made you well. Go in peace."

I drew strength from a second passage, **Luke 7:1-10**. This one deals with the tremendous faith of the Centurion, or Roman Officer. He had a prized servant who was ill to the point of death, and he sent some representatives to bring Jesus to his home to heal the servant.

Jesus was on his way, but before he arrived, the Centurion sent other friends to ask that Jesus merely speak the word, because the Centurion didn't feel worthy of troubling Jesus, and he knew that merely a word from Him would be sufficient to heal his servant.

The Centurion's faith was so great, Jesus marveled at it. Imagine doing something so amazing that it would make the Lord Jesus marvel!

> "The Centurion's faith was so great, Jesus marveled at it."

Jesus fulfilled the Centurion's request, and the servant was indeed healed. Once again, an example of the extreme power of unbridled faith in God.

> **Luke 7:1-10 (NKJV)**
>
> Now when He concluded all His sayings in the hearing of the people, He entered Capernaum. ²And a certain centurion's servant, who was dear to him, was sick and ready to die. ³So when he heard about Jesus, he sent elders of the Jews to Him, pleading with Him to come and heal his servant. ⁴And when they came to Jesus, they begged Him earnestly, saying that the one for whom He should do this was deserving, ⁵ "for he loves our nation, and has built us a synagogue."

⁶ Then Jesus went with them. And when He was already not far from the house, the centurion sent friends to Him, saying to Him, "Lord, do not trouble Yourself, for I am not worthy that You should enter under my roof. ⁷ Therefore I did not even think myself worthy to come to You. But say the word, and my servant will be healed. ⁸ For I also am a man placed under authority, having soldiers under me. And I say to one, 'Go,' and he goes; and to another, 'Come,' and he comes; and to my servant, 'Do this,' and he does it."

⁹ When Jesus heard these things, He marveled at him, and turned around and said to the crowd that followed Him, "I say to you, I have not found such great faith, not even in Israel!" ¹⁰ And those who were sent, returning to the house, found the servant well who had been sick.

Scripture taken from the New King James Version®. Copyright © 1982 by Thomas Nelson. Used by permission. All rights reserved.

I was awed and inspired by this story. The Centurion's faith became a model for me to follow.

> "The Centurion's faith became a model for me to follow."

The third scripture reference that served as a revelation to me was **Luke 11:1-13**. In this passage, Jesus is giving lessons to his disciples on how to pray. In the beginning of the passage, he teaches them in general terms about prayer.

This, however, is just scratching the surface of how we are to proceed with our communication with God.

After he gives them the model prayer in verses 2-4, he delves further in the following verses to teach them more about prayer, and about what their mindset should be when they are making requests of the Father.

As I read these verses, I became overwhelmed with the message Jesus was conveying to his disciples. Ask. We must know specifically what it is that we want and need, and WE MUST ASK. We must also be persistent when asking. ***Ask***, and you will receive. ***Seek*** and you will find. ***Knock*** and the door will be opened.

I was completely blown away by this.

Because I had grown up in the church and memorized scripture as a child, I had probably read that scripture passage dozens of times. But none hit me so profoundly as that time when I realized how much it applied to my situation.

> "We must know specifically what it is that we want and need, and WE MUST ASK."

These verses hit me right where I lived, and they changed my entire outlook. I could ask God to send the Holy Spirit to be with me through this whole thing. God promised me He would send that version of Himself to comfort me, heal me, and bring me peace.

I had only to ask for it.

I clung to that promise, and prayed fervently for the Holy Spirit to dwell with me and get me through the surgery and the healing process. It was an amazing realization for me.

Luke 11:1-13 (NLT)

Once Jesus was in a certain place praying. As he finished, one of his disciples came to him and said, "Lord, teach us to pray, just as John taught his disciples."

[2] Jesus said, "This is how you should pray:

"Father, may your name be kept holy.
  May your Kingdom come soon.
[3] Give us each day the food we need,
[4] and forgive us our sins,
  as we forgive those who sin against us.
And don't let us yield to temptation."

[5] Then, teaching them more about prayer, he used this story: "Suppose you went to a friend's house at midnight, wanting to borrow three loaves of bread. You say to him, [6] 'A friend of mine has just arrived for a visit, and I have nothing for him to eat.' [7] And suppose he calls out from his bedroom, 'Don't bother me. The door is locked for the night, and my family and I are all in bed. I can't help you.' [8] But I tell you this—though he won't do it for friendship's sake, if you keep knocking long enough, he will get up and give you whatever you need because of your shameless persistence.

[9] "And so I tell you, keep on asking, and you will receive what you ask for. Keep on seeking, and you will find. Keep on knocking, and the door will be opened to you. [10] For everyone who asks, receives. Everyone who seeks, finds. And to everyone who knocks, the door will be opened.

[11] "You fathers—if your children ask for a fish, do you give them a snake instead? [12] Or if they ask for an egg, do you give them a scorpion? Of course not! [13] So if you sinful people know how to give good gifts to your children, how much more will your heavenly Father give the Holy Spirit to those who ask him.

I have to admit, I was ready for some shameless persistence.

The fourth passage, **Luke 13:6-9,** is the parable of the barren fig tree. This one had a huge impact on my thinking because it added some perspective for me on *why* this whole thing might be happening.

The owner of a garden had planted a fig tree, and was annoyed that the tree had not produced fruit for three years. He ordered the caretaker to cut it down, because he was tired of finding the tree barren year after year.

But the caretaker asked for a reprieve for the tree. He wanted to give it some extra care and attention by digging around it and fertilizing it. The caretaker knew this would be a necessary process to help the fig tree grow and produce fruit for the owner.

> "He wanted to give {the fig tree} some extra care and attention by digging around it and fertilizing it."

Luke 13:6-9 (NLT)

⁶Then Jesus told this story: "A man planted a fig tree in his garden and came again and again to see if there was any fruit on it, but he was always disappointed. ⁷Finally, he said to his gardener, 'I've waited three years, and there hasn't been a single fig! Cut it down. It's just taking up space in the garden.'

⁸"The gardener answered, 'Sir, give it one more chance. Leave it another year, and I'll give it special attention and plenty of fertilizer. ⁹If we get figs next year, fine. If not, then you can cut it down.'"

Wow. I was dumbfounded by this story.

So was that it? Was I a fig tree?

I had not considered that before. Here again, I had probably read and heard that passage many times throughout my life, but no time of hearing or reading had the impact on me as this moment when I realized what God was communicating in this simple parable.

These verses explained to me *why* bad things happen to us, and why we must sometimes weather storms in our lives.

> *"These verses explained to me why bad things happen to us, and why we must sometimes weather storms in our lives."*

I realized that we all must go through a sort of "fertilization" process sometimes in order to grow and produce fruit for the kingdom of God. Otherwise, we would be stagnant, stuck in the same place our whole lives.

Never learning. Never growing.

Yes, that was it. I was most definitely being fertilized.

Food for Thought

Have you ever wondered why bad things happen to good people?

Or better yet, why are bad things happening to me?

Perhaps God is using your difficult or dire circumstances to "fertilize" your soil and help you grow.

It can be hard to admit that we would need such fertilization. It was certainly hard for me, but if we are all truthful with ourselves, we would realize that stagnation in our prayer lives, and in our Christian journeys with God, happens on a regular basis.

> "Perhaps God is using your difficult or dire circumstances to "fertilize" your soil and help you grow."

I know I have been complacent at times. It's easy to fall into the trap. I get busy with my life. Things hum along and go pretty smoothly. I periodically forget from where and from Whom my blessings flow. But then He allows me to experience those trials that eventually lead me right back to Him.

It's the only way we can truly grow and mature.

7

PRAYING SPECIFICALLY

A WHIRLWIND OF EMOTIONS AND events seemed to be engulfing me. So much happened in such a short time, close to three weeks. I gained knowledge and understanding that I never would have gained had I not gone through that experience. I also gained a closeness with my Creator that I never had before.

I learned that I should pray specifically for the outcome I wanted to see, and to pray for God's hand and Holy Spirit to guide the physicians who would perform the surgery I needed. I determined to have absolute, unwavering faith in God to do what I needed Him to do. I needed to stay here for my children and for my husband, and I needed to be healthy.

What next, then?

I had learned so much from studying the book of Luke, not only with my Bible study group, but also certainly during my own study time. How, then, could I apply all the knowledge I had gained to my situation?

How was I going to pray specifically?

At first, I didn't even know what to pray for, but as I studied and went to my doctor visits, what I should ask Him for became clear to me.

> *"...what I should ask Him for became clear to me."*

I started out by brainstorming and listing the key items I wanted to see happen. After I thought about it just a little bit, it was not a difficult list to compose. I shared this list with my husband and close family, and with our friends who were praying for me.

I began to pray earnestly for these *seven* outcomes:

1. Not to die (Obvious, but had to be stated)

2. For the tumor to be benign, non-cancerous

3. For the surgeons to be able to remove the tumor completely, while leaving the pituitary gland intact

4. To regain any eyesight I had lost

5. Not to have to take medications for this for the rest of my life, due to the tumor secretions, nor to need radiation treatments, which I had been told were a possibility, and would complicate things even further

6. Overall and complete healing from the surgery and the awful condition of acromegaly
7. To be able to get pregnant again and carry the baby to full term

Number 7 on the list—to get pregnant again and carry to full term, was very closely tied to, and dependent upon, item number 3—for the surgeons to remove the whole tumor while leaving the gland intact. It would be extremely difficult, if not impossible, to have a healthy pregnancy without a pituitary gland. It provides the necessary hormone secretions to keep that delicate balance needed to sustain a pregnancy.

So item three was a big one.

> "It would be extremely difficult, if not impossible, to have a healthy pregnancy without a pituitary gland."

Even though it was still top priority for me to have another baby, Dr. Hays was not encouraged about the odds. Well, we would see.

I had a weapon: Specific Prayer.

And I was going to use it.

Food for Thought

Has anyone ever heard this prayer/rhyme?:
> Now I lay me down to sleep,
>> I pray the Lord my soul to keep.
>
> And if I die before I wake,
>> I pray the Lord my soul to take.*

Or how about this one?
> God is great; God is good.
>> Let us thank Him for our food.
>
> By His hands, we all are fed,
>> Give us, Lord, our daily bread.*

*These works are in the public domain.

Many children have been taught to pray in the aforementioned manner. Rhymes. Generalities. And that is okay. We should teach children to pray and be thankful for their blessings. But often after we reach adulthood, we fail to progress beyond learning those rote prayers. We go through the motions of praying without really knowing the meaning of, or even thinking about, what we are saying. We recite prayers, or say the same thing again and again without being tuned in to what God wants to hear from us.

To many of us, this is praying.

It could also be wasted opportunity.

> "We go through the motions of praying without really knowing the meaning, or even thinking about what we are saying."

Remember the great power of prayer we discussed earlier. Powerful prayer that altered the heavens and the elements. Power we have at our disposal if we follow God's instructions on how to use it.

Another example from the Bible of effective, specific prayer that cannot be overlooked is the one in which Abraham sends his faithful servant to his homeland to seek a bride for his son, Isaac. The servant prays very specifically for a sign so he will know which young woman God wants him to choose. The entire account is found in **Genesis 24**. The passage of **Genesis 24:12-20** details the servant's prayer, and God's amazing, swift response.

> **Genesis 24:12-20 (NLT)**
>
> [12] "O Lord, God of my master, Abraham," he prayed. "Please give me success today, and show unfailing love to my master, Abraham. [13] See, I am standing here beside this spring, and the young women of the town are coming out to draw water. [14] This is my request. I will ask one of them, 'Please give me a drink from your jug.' If she says, 'Yes, have a drink, and I will water your camels, too!'—let her be the one you have selected as Isaac's wife. This is how I will know that you have shown unfailing love to my master."

> [15] Before he had finished praying, he saw a young woman named Rebekah coming out with her water jug on her shoulder. She was the daughter of Bethuel, who was the son of Abraham's brother Nahor and his wife, Milcah. [16] Rebekah was very beautiful and old enough to be married, but she was still a virgin. She went down to the spring, filled her jug, and came up again. [17] Running over to her, the servant said, "Please give me a little drink of water from your jug."
>
> [18] "Yes, my lord," she answered, "have a drink." And she quickly lowered her jug from her shoulder and gave him a drink. [19] When she had given him a drink, she said, "I'll draw water for your camels, too, until they have had enough to drink." [20] So she quickly emptied her jug into the watering trough and ran back to the well to draw water for all his camels.

Verse 15 states that before the words were completely out of the servant's mouth, he saw the young woman God would use to fulfill his request.

I want to encourage you to take a deep dive into the passages in Luke that I have outlined in the previous chapter, especially the ones pertaining to prayer and the way to approach it. Read them. Study them. Ask God to help you apply them to your life and circumstances.

You will be amazed at how richly your life will be blessed when you learn to move beyond the standard prayers of childhood and into a real, conversing relationship with God the Father. Studying His Word will clearly bring you closer to Him, because you will be reading words He penned just for the purpose of telling us what He expects from us, and words that allow Him to speak directly to each individual person who is blessed enough to read them.

8

GOD ANSWERS PRAYER
(AND HE DRIVES A PICKUP TRUCK)

A FUNNY THING HAPPENED ON our Sunday afternoon drive to the hospital. You will recall the passage of **Luke 7:1-10** about the Centurion. I had been pondering that story every day, and determining I was going to have faith comparable to that of the Centurion.

During that trip, I was talking with my husband, Don, and we were discussing, among other things, the surgery that would take place the following morning. My parents were to care for our children that night, and my dear friend Lori would keep them the next day so my parents could visit me.

I hated being away from Jacquelyn and Graham, and I was understandably apprehensive about the impending surgery. I was beginning to feel scared, inadequate, and overwhelmed.

I needed a faith booster.

> "I was beginning to feel scared, inadequate, and overwhelmed."

We were driving east on I-40 and had just gotten into the busy Nashville traffic. There were multiple lanes at this point, and we were in one of the middle lanes.

At that moment, I looked up and saw a gleaming white, very clean, dual-wheeled pickup truck zooming past us in the lane to our left. Behind each set of dual tires on the rear of the truck was a set of shiny, clean, silver mud flaps. The afternoon sun was low in the sky behind us and reflected brightly off the mud flaps. We couldn't help but notice them. What word do you suppose was emblazoned in chrome on both of those mud flaps?

You guessed it. CENTURION.

I pointed and exclaimed to Don, and we both laughed out loud in utter amazement. We knew that truck was meant for us to see. I guess you could call that a Tennessee redneck miracle! But I loved it. It was just what I needed.

We arrived at the hospital in Nashville, and I settled into a holding room for overnight patients who were there for early morning surgery. That evening, we reviewed the specific prayer list, and prayed over each item. It was down to the wire now, and the time had come to put my faith into practice.

> *"It was down to the wire now, and the time had come to put my faith into practice."*

November 3, 1997 was a Monday morning. I have never minded Mondays too much, but this one I admit I dreaded. I had an ever so tiny glimpse of how Jesus might have felt when He prayed in the Garden of Gethsemane, as recorded in **Matthew 26:39**, to let this cup pass from Him. It was stressful, but certainly nothing close to what Jesus was facing. I felt God going with me every step of the way.

Matthew 26:36-39 (NLT)

36 Then Jesus went with them to the olive grove called Gethsemane, and he said, "Sit here while I go over there to pray." 37 He took Peter and Zebedee's two sons, James and John, and he became anguished and distressed. 38 He told them, "My soul is crushed with grief to the point of death. Stay here and keep watch with me."

39 He went on a little farther and bowed with his face to the ground, praying, "My Father! If it is possible, let this cup of suffering be taken away from me. Yet I want your will to be done, not mine."

> *"I felt God going with me every step of the way."*

I am not sure how many hours I was under. Maybe three or four. I do remember waking to see my husband standing anxiously over me. He watched me closely as I came out of my groggy, anesthetized state, my breathing labored. All I remember was that I wanted to take a good, deep breath. It was finally over. The surgery I had dreaded and prayed over and agonized over was just that. Over. What a relief.

Now it was time to recuperate.

Later, Don told me about the meeting the neurosurgeon had with him and my parents after my surgery was over. He told them things went much better and easier than they had anticipated. He thought he had gotten the whole tumor out, and he was able to leave the gland in place. It looked a bit squashed from sitting under the tumor for so long, but he felt like it might recover fairly well. And he was optimistic about my ability to avoid radiation. They would need to perform another MRI in a day or two to see how everything looked.

I was in the hospital for a total of five days, Monday through Friday. On Wednesday, my doctor gave the order for me to have that follow-up MRI. This time, my sweet husband was right there with me, and waiting when I came out of that awful tunnel. The results looked favorable, as the doctor had anticipated after the surgery, and my recovery was off and running.

So far, the specific prayer list was looking good. I was still alive, which was the number one request on the list. Also, the biopsy results had shown that the tumor was indeed benign. Whew! Thank God for a "Yes" on item number two.

Over the next few days and weeks, we would learn even more about how God was answering our prayers.

> "Over the next few days and weeks, we would learn even more about how God was answering our prayers."

During a post-op visit with the neurosurgeon, he shared the results of the follow-up MRI I'd had right after the surgery. It revealed that he was indeed able to get the entire tumor out of my head and leave the pituitary gland completely intact. It just so happened that the tumor had been sitting on top of the gland in an accessible position, rather than being wrapped around it, thus making the tumor easier to remove. He said the pituitary gland looked really good, and he saw no reason why normal pituitary function could not return.

We were thanking God for the mighty "Yes" to item number three on the list. That was a big one.

Next was a second visit to the neuro-ophthalmologist a couple weeks after surgery to recheck my eyesight. During the first visit, he concluded from my tests that I was losing my peripheral vision. It was eventually going to become more and more tunnel-like and lead to blindness if the tumor had been allowed to stay. During the second visit, after the surgery, the tests showed the peripheral vision I had lost had been completely restored! Since the optic nerves were no longer being perilously stretched by the tumor, my eyesight had returned to normal. God was so good! Check off item four.

Did I dare ask for more?

He told us in His word to ask, right there in **Luke 11:9**. It would be disobedient not to, so ask I did.

> *"It would be disobedient not to, so ask I did."*

Number five on the list may seem petty to some people, especially people who do have to be on medication permanently. But I knew if I wanted to become pregnant and carry a healthy baby to full term, I would not need to have extra medicines or chemicals in my body. Also, the possibility of damage to the gland was too much of a risk if radiation were introduced to the equation.

The doctors told us all the changes that must occur during pregnancy are almost too complex to manage chemically or artificially with medicines; therefore, normal, natural pituitary function would be necessary to support a healthy pregnancy. That would best be accomplished if the gland were in place, fully functional, and there were no medications or radiation involved.

I consulted with Dr. Hays a few weeks after the surgery. She ran several blood tests to be sure the growth hormone levels were dropping. They were, and because I was doing so well, she saw no reason to put me on any medication other than the temporary stuff right after the surgery. And because there appeared to be no remaining traces of the tumor, radiation was no longer being considered.

Item number five on the list had been granted another "Yes" from God. I was reeling with joy.

I will never forget the day, not long after that, when I had another follow-up visit with Dr. Hays. She had been studying my post-op MRI, my blood test results, my eye test results, and my accounts of how much better I was feeling. It was all rather surprising to her. Patients with this kind of problem, acromegaly from a growth hormone secreting tumor, traditionally don't do so well.

> "Patients with this kind of problem ... traditionally don't do so well."

She looked at me, and the look on her face was a mixture of surprise, bewilderment, disbelief, and even delight. Her words were music to my ears.
"It appears that…you're cured."
Item six was knocked out of the park.

Food for Thought

During this time when God was so consistently answering our prayers in the affirmative, I was joyful and thankful for what He had done for me, but I cautioned against being surprised at the results. Had I been surprised, I believe it would have been an indication that my faith was not as strong as it should have been.

> *"...I was joyful and thankful for what He had done for me, but I cautioned against being surprised at the results."*

Thinking in these terms reminded me of **Acts 12:6-17**. It is the account of Peter's imprisonment, and the group of Christians who had gathered to pray for his release.

While this group was still praying, Peter showed up at the outer gate of the house where they were praying and began knocking. A young girl heard him speak and recognized his voice and, in her excitement, she left him standing there while she ran and told the group. They scoffed at the idea of Peter being there, and said she must be out of her mind. She persisted, and when the group learned it truly was Peter, they were nothing short of amazed.

Did their amazement reflect a lack of faith, or just astoundment at the speed with which God can choose to grant our petitions? Sometimes we have to wait on Him, but sometimes His answers are so swift, they catch us completely by surprise.

Acts 12:6-17 (NLT)

⁶ The night before Peter was to be placed on trial, he was asleep, fastened with two chains between two soldiers. Others stood guard at the prison gate. ⁷ Suddenly, there was a bright light in the cell, and an angel of the Lord stood before Peter. The angel struck him on the side to awaken him and said, "Quick! Get up!" And the chains fell off his wrists. ⁸ Then the angel told him, "Get dressed and put on your sandals." And he did. "Now put on your coat and follow me," the angel ordered.

⁹ So Peter left the cell, following the angel. But all the time he thought it was a vision. He didn't realize it was actually happening. ¹⁰ They passed the first and second guard posts and came to the iron gate leading to the city, and this opened for them all by itself. So they passed through and started walking down the street, and then the angel suddenly left him.

¹¹ Peter finally came to his senses. "It's really true!" he said. "The Lord has sent his angel and saved me from Herod and from what the Jewish leaders had planned to do to me!"

¹² When he realized this, he went to the home of Mary, the mother of John Mark, where many were gathered for prayer. ¹³ He knocked at the door in the gate, and a servant girl named Rhoda came to open it. ¹⁴ When she

recognized Peter's voice, she was so overjoyed that, instead of opening the door, she ran back inside and told everyone, "Peter is standing at the door!"

¹⁵ "You're out of your mind!" they said. When she insisted, they decided, "It must be his angel."

¹⁶ Meanwhile, Peter continued knocking. When they finally opened the door and saw him, they were amazed. ¹⁷ He motioned for them to quiet down and told them how the Lord had led him out of prison. "Tell James and the other brothers what happened," he said. And then he went to another place.

Don't ever be shocked when God keeps His word.

9

LET IT GO

IT WAS AUGUST OF 2000. We had since left Waverly and moved to Franklin, Kentucky two years prior because my husband had taken a job there. I missed my Tuesday morning Bible study group in Waverly.

A ladies' Bible study was in the process of starting at our current church, and I was anxious to join. I had heard great things about the particular course they had chosen, and it seemed like a good opportunity to become involved in a meaningful study with the ladies at our church in Franklin.

It had been nearly three years since my tumor surgery. I thanked God every day for answering all those prayers, for showing me what to pray for, and for showing me how to pray specifically for the outcomes that I needed.

I was living my life as I had hoped and prayed I could. I was alive, and physically able to take care of my family, and for that I was truly thankful. Six out of the seven items on my list had been fulfilled. It was really more than I ever deserved. I was so very grateful to God for the abundant ways He had blessed me.

Still, that nagging desire to become pregnant again was strong. There was another baby who was supposed to be. There had to be. I could picture her in my mind. It was what I wanted most. I was unwilling to let go of that vision.

> "There was another baby who was supposed to be ... I was unwilling to let go of that vision."

For two years and nine months I prayed for God to answer that seventh request. But the answer was "No." I refused to give in to what seemed to be unfolding as God's will. Why could I not have what I wanted? I was cured. It should happen.

"Won't you be happy and content with what I have given you already?" I felt like He was asking me.

"Of course I will," was my reply.

But nothing changed in my heart. He knew I did not mean it, and God knows the heart of each individual, as David so eloquently states in **Psalm 139:1-6**. I couldn't fool God. He knew I was still gripped by my own stubborn will.

Psalm 139:1-6 (NLT)

¹ O Lord, you have examined my heart
and know everything about me.

² You know when I sit down or stand up.
   You know my thoughts even when I'm
far away.
³ You see me when I travel
   and when I rest at home.
   You know everything I do.
⁴ You know what I am going to say
   even before I say it, Lord.
⁵ You go before me and follow me.
   You place your hand of blessing on my head.
⁶ Such knowledge is too wonderful for me,
   too great for me to understand!

> "I couldn't fool God. He knew I was still gripped by my own stubborn will."

Then one of our Bible study lessons (again, no coincidence, I'm sure) hit me between the eyes. It was about struggling with your role in God's kingdom, something I do frequently. The text stated that only God's chosen task for you will ultimately satisfy, and that you should not wait until it is too late to realize the privilege of serving Him in the position He has chosen for you.

That was a huge realization for me. I had been approaching my Seventh Request to God all wrong. It was based on what I wanted, rather than seeking God's true will for me and for our family. My will and my desires had to take a back seat to God's will. If I were truly His child, I would defer to His judgment, and accept what His future held for me, because God knows the position He has for me. I had to remember that His grace was sufficient.

> *"My will and my desires had to take a back seat to God's will."*

That's it, then. I was weary of constantly swimming upstream. I was so emotionally exhausted from worrying and obsessing about what I wanted, and I was blind to the things God was trying to show me. He wanted me to know how important it was to appreciate the family I had, and to completely trust Him with our future.

Once I came to that realization, I finally, genuinely let go and trusted Him to be the author of my future. Whether I became pregnant again or not, I told God I would be happy. It was fully in His hands now.

This time I meant it.

10

Ecstasy & Agony

September 29, 2000 was a Friday. It happened to be the Friday before my kids' fall break from school, and we had planned a beach trip with my mother and dad. I couldn't wait to get down there. We all loved the beach, and Don desperately needed a vacation from his job. Lately it had been particularly hectic and stressful. We planned to load everything up and hit the road as soon as Jacquelyn and Graham were home from school.

The Seventh Request

I had been feeling a little funny in my lower abdomen for a couple of days. When I moved a certain way, there was a slight pulling down low on the right side. I was familiar with that feeling, but guarding against getting my hopes up too much. Since I had resolved a few weeks earlier to let go and put God in the driver's seat, I was prepared for whatever might happen. Still, I decided to make a trip to the store to pick up a pregnancy test, just in case. Since we were leaving on a trip, I wanted to find out for sure what was going on.

> "Since I had resolved a few weeks earlier to let go and put God in the driver's seat, I was prepared for whatever might happen."

My anticipation was building. When I got home from the store, I wasted no time, and performed the test immediately. To my joy and sheer delight, it was positive!

I was astounded and amazed at God's grace and kindness. I dropped to my knees and prayed, thanking Him for His willingness to allow the beginning of a "Yes" to my Seventh Request.

The crazy realization hit me. All that time I was bent on having things my own way. My stubborn will, my plan. Instead, I just needed to let go and allow God to have control.

I was so excited I had to call Don. I asked him to come home right away because I needed to talk with him. I knew he was very busy, but what I had to say was very important. With our plans to get on the road immediately after the children were home from school, I did not know when else I would be able to tell him the news in a private setting.

Besides, I was about to explode with elation and I wanted to tell him right then.

It was about ten in the morning when he arrived at home. Fortunately, we only lived about a mile from his work. Even still, I could hardly wait for him to get home. I met him at the door, and as soon as he walked in, I shared the news with him. He was thrilled, and so sweet because he knew, of course, what I had been struggling with.

We hugged and held each other for a long time; then we sat down briefly together to have a short conversation about this new turn of events, and we discussed the best time to tell Jacquelyn and Graham they were going to have a baby brother or sister. We thought telling them and my parents at the beach would be wonderful. What a fun, special vacation this was going to be!

Finally, we prayed together and thanked God for His unfailing grace and mercy, for His ability to heal and make us whole, and for His willingness to answer our prayers—for His willingness to fulfill our Seventh Request.

> "...we prayed together and thanked God for His unfailing grace and mercy, for ... His willingness to fulfill our Seventh Request."

Our happy moment was all too short. Don had to head on back to work right away if we were going to get on the road at a good time that afternoon, so I kissed him goodbye and shifted my gears back toward preparing for our trip. For the next two or three hours, I continued with packing and getting everything ready to go.

That was when I got the call.

Don's brother, David, was on the other end. I remember being so confused when he started speaking to me. I could scarcely take in what he was saying. Something about his mother calling him and being hysterical, and something else about his dad—and a gunshot. He did not have all the details yet, and he would call me back when he did.

When I hung up the phone with David, all I could think was, "It's probably all right. There is just some misunderstanding. He will call back soon and tell me everything is okay." I tried very hard to stay calm and not worry.

But when he called again, I knew everything was not going to be okay. In fact, everything was about to fall completely apart. Don's sweet father had turned a gun to his head and pulled the trigger.

> *"...everything was about to fall completely apart."*

I've never spent another day in my life like that one, and I hope I never do again. I felt like I had been punched in the stomach. I went from elation to agony in just a few hours. It was hard to believe we had been so ecstatically happy just that morning.

Now the happiness was gone.

My brain was on overload. I couldn't believe it. This couldn't be happening. What should I do next? Obviously, I needed to get in touch with Don again and tell him to come back home. This was before he had a cell phone, and contacting him was difficult when he was out of his office. Of course, he was out in the plant, and away from his desk. I sent him a message through the switchboard operator to call home as soon as possible. I also had people in the plant out looking for him. This was definitely an emergency.

After what seemed like an eternity, Don finally called me, assuming I was contacting him about what we had discussed earlier that morning. But when I told him the details of my phone call with David, he was astonished, heartbroken, and in shock. He rushed back home and called his brother. They talked for several minutes. Bit by bit, we began to piece together what had happened that afternoon. It was more than we could comprehend.

> "Bit by bit, we began to piece together what had happened that afternoon. It was more than we could comprehend."

His father was still alive, and had been taken to the hospital in Memphis, Tennessee. Their mother had also been taken to the same hospital, after suffering what appeared to be a heart attack. Some other family members were with them until we could all get down there.

The whole scenario was what nightmares are made of. I kept thinking, "I am going to wake up and find that this is all just some horrid dream." But I did not wake up.

I went to pick up Jacquelyn and Graham from school. The tears made it hard to see to drive. I had to explain to them, as briefly and as tactfully as I could to two young children, the reason we weren't going to the beach. I told them Grandpa had had "an accident."

We were already packed for our trip, so we loaded up the children and all our luggage. Instead of heading southeast to the beach, we headed southwest to Memphis.

It was a long drive.

Food for Thought

Blindsided—again?

Just when you think it's safe to relax and enjoy life, something else can hit you harder than before, and catch you completely off guard.

Even though I had been through all that I had with the brain tumor and learning about how to pray specifically, I almost felt like I was starting from square one.

> "...I almost felt like I was starting from square one."

I have to admit, I did not fall into the groove of praying specifically right away after this last calamity. I was in such a state of shock, it took me a few weeks to compose myself, and to be able to cope personally with what was happening. I also knew I had to hold everything together for Jacquelyn and Graham, for my poor, over-stressed husband, and for my unborn baby.

I think God is patient with us when we experience events that have that kind of effect on us. He knows the limits of our humanness, and He waits patiently for us to realize that He hasn't gone anywhere. He is still by our side.

Sometimes He is a lot closer than we think.

11

A Bigger Fig Tree

Over the course of the next many weeks, in addition to juggling his responsibilities at work, Don was constantly on the road to Memphis and back to help out however he could, and to spend time by his dad's side. He had been moved from the hospital to a nursing home in Memphis, and we did not know how long he could hang on like he was.

I stayed home and took care of our children, all the while feeling miserable and sick, both physically and emotionally. Morning sickness had set in, and true to my past experiences, the dreadful, nagging nausea was not confined just to morning.

On the Saturday night preceding the morning of Jacquelyn's birthday in December, Don had been in Memphis to visit his dad. He drove back home to be there for her special day. The phone rang early the next morning, and it was the phone call we had been dreading. In the wee hours of that morning, the day of Jacquelyn's eighth birthday, Don's dad passed away.

> "The phone rang early the next morning, and it was the phone call we had been dreading."

He had developed a staph infection, and it was too much for him to fight off. For two and a half months he held on. I don't see how. He was a strong person, but sometimes strong people get to the end of their strength, and he had gotten to the end of his.

Apparently, he had suffered from depression. He was a World War II veteran, and he had served as a medic in the army. At the tender age of 21, he had experienced and survived the atrocities at the Battle of the Bulge, and other tours on the European warfront. Because of his war tenure, he had posttraumatic stress disorder, suffering flashbacks and nightmares frequently. We knew this, but we did not know exactly the extent of his problems. He also had suffered a terrible accident a few years before which took away most of the use of his left arm. Many things contributed to his fragile state of mind, and he finally reached a breaking point.

Needless to say, stress like what we had experienced over the past couple of months is very bad for a pregnant woman, especially when she is in the very early stages of pregnancy. I was upset all the time. With all that was happening with my father-in-law and the stress my husband was under, I felt guilty for worrying about myself.

Actually, I was not worried about me at all. I was worried about our baby. I was terrified of having a third miscarriage, especially after everything I had gone through to bring this precious life into existence.

I could not lose this baby!

> "I was terrified of having a third miscarriage, especially after everything I had gone through to bring this precious life into existence."

I also felt guilty for my anger and resentment over the fact that our happiness for this pregnancy had been ripped away from us before we even had a chance to think about it, and certainly before we had a chance to enjoy it. I thought about Don's poor dad and all that he had suffered, and I felt even worse.

The passage of **Luke 13:6-9** about the fig tree and the fertilization process came flooding back to me. Why was I being dug around and fertilized—again?

Just how large and fruitful did this fig tree need to be anyway?

Food for Thought

Instead of viewing life as a collection of good events punctuated with some bad or painful experiences, or vice versa, I have learned to view it as just—life.

Our whole lives consist of a series of experiences, all strung together by the time we spend on this earth. God often allows things to happen based on the choices that we and others have made, whether those choices were recent or long ago, and the things that follow are what we are left to cope with and manage.

> "God often allows things to happen based on the choices that we and others have made..."

Sometimes things happen that are in our control, but many times they certainly are not. Those can be the hardest to deal with and understand. When those things inevitably show up, refer often to the scripture passages discussed earlier in this book. Use them to jumpstart your prayer life.

I would even suggest keeping a written record of your requests and petitions to God. It is a great way to document the blessings you receive, and to share with others what God has done in your life. Getting on track with a diligent, regular prayer and Bible study regimen will increase your ability to handle everything "life" throws at you.

It's been the one thing that has gotten me through it all.

My Requests

The Seventh Request

My Requests

My Requests

The Seventh Request

My Requests

My Requests

The Seventh Request

My Requests

My Requests

12

SPECIFIC PRAYER—
ROUND TWO

MY DECEMBER PRENATAL DOCTOR visit took place very shortly after Don's father's funeral. I had recently gotten past the end of the first trimester, around the 14th to 15th week, and thankfully the morning sickness had abated.

After the doctor examined me, she asked if I had been experiencing any pain. Actually, I had noticed some slight pain recently while I was attempting to do a few exercises, and I told her about it.

She nodded and said, "You've been contracting. You need to stay off your feet until the end of your pregnancy. I won't put you on strict bed rest—yet—but you need to make an effort to rest and sit or lie down as much as you can."

What? What do you mean I have to stay off my feet? I have a second grader and a kindergartener. My husband works half the time and is gone the other half of the time dealing with the aftermath of the past two and a half months. Holy cow, this is December. How on earth am I supposed to stay in bed or on the sofa until the end of May?

It seemed impossible. I was, after all, only one person. I couldn't clone myself, and there were some things that I had to handle. But the doctor told me if I wanted to carry this baby to full term, and I desperately did, then I was going to have to comply with her orders as much as I possibly could.

Another well-timed scripture passage that came to my mind when I needed it most was the one in which Jesus tells his disciples that nothing is impossible with God, **Matthew 19:26.** He tells them that even though some things might seem humanly impossible, with God, *all things* are possible.

> He tells them that even though some things might seem humanly impossible, with God, all things are possible.

Matthew 19:21-26 (NLT)

²¹ Jesus told him, "If you want to be perfect, go and sell all your possessions and give the money to the poor, and you will have treasure in heaven. Then come, follow me."

²² But when the young man heard this, he went away sad, for he had many possessions.

²³ Then Jesus said to his disciples, "I tell you the truth, it is very hard for a rich person to enter the Kingdom of Heaven. ²⁴ I'll say it again—it is easier for a camel to go through the eye of a needle than for a rich person to enter the Kingdom of God!"

²⁵ The disciples were astounded. "Then who in the world can be saved?" they asked.

²⁶ Jesus looked at them intently and said, "Humanly speaking, it is impossible. But with God everything is possible."

I was feeling massively overwhelmed, so I decided it was time to dump all of this at the Lord's feet—again. I had become so burdened with everything, that I got away from the peace I had experienced three years before. How could I have done such a thing? No wonder God was fertilizing me. It was time, once again, to get down on my fluid-retentive knees and start praying.

> "I was feeling massively overwhelmed, so I decided it was time to dump all of this at the Lord's feet—again."

I needed a new specific prayer list. God had knocked out the other one in superior fashion, and according to His Word, I should bring my new set of petitions to Him. So I did.

I wrote out a new list of requests to pray for. I guess you could call this the addendum or sub-list for my Seventh Request on the earlier list. This one wasn't as long, but equally important. It was easy to figure out what I wanted this time. Very straightforward. Instead of praying for my own life, this time I was petitioning Him on behalf of my unborn child. I felt even more passionate about this round of specific prayer.

My new specific prayer list:

- That my stress level would go down and that I could remain calm and happy for the remainder of my pregnancy—for my baby's sake and for the sake of my other two children.

- That the baby would be healthy and have no problems. Since I was turning 36, I was worried about all kinds of issues.

- That I carry this baby to full term. Her being born prematurely would add even more risks to an already tenuous and stressful situation. I just wanted this pregnancy to become as normal as possible.

> "I felt even more passionate about this round of specific prayer."

Every morning I would wake up and breathe a prayer of thanks and a sigh of relief. One more day behind us. Each passing day marked progress. Every time I spoke with my mother and dad on the phone, my dad would exclaim, "Another week down! Only ____ more to go!" Fill in the blank with wherever we were at that point. We were especially happy to reach the half way mark at 20 weeks.

The doctor scheduled an ultrasound at this point, in late January. I had been vigorously applying that specific prayer list, and I was very anxious to see how everything looked, and to find out whether the baby was a boy or a girl. We always wanted to find out. I couldn't stand not knowing, especially if it was possible to know. Remember how I don't like surprises, unless it's flowers or chocolate. Not to mention, I had to know what color afghan to crochet.

We anxiously surveyed the monitor as the ultrasound technician ran the probe over my bulging belly. There SHE was! It was a girl, and she looked perfect! Her little features were so distinct, and I gazed at her in amazement, pondering how far this little one had come, while she had no idea.

> "...I gazed at her in amazement, pondering how far this little one had come, while she had no idea."

The next milestone was reaching the 24-week mark. That was particularly huge. I read a lot during that time because it was one thing I could do. The 24-week point in the pregnancy was important, according to the reading, because the statistical odds of a baby surviving outside the womb increased dramatically at that point. That brought more peace to my mind, but I had been praying fervently for my list, and I had assurance in my heart that the Lord would answer my prayer to let her be full term.

Staying off her feet for months on end is difficult for any pregnant woman, but it's especially true if she already has a family. My husband helped whenever he could, but there were some things that I just had to do. I would take my kids to school and pick them up, cook, do very limited grocery shopping, and I taught a Sunday school class at church. It was easy for me to prepare the lessons. I had lots of down time.

The hardest part of that endeavor was climbing the stairs at church, a prospect I dreaded each week. I knew EXACTLY how many stairs there were, because I counted each one every time I ascended them. In hindsight, it would have been smart to request a meeting room for my class downstairs!

Before that experience, I didn't realize how debilitating inactivity could be to a person. Too much sitting, too much reclining, and too much rest all contribute to low energy levels and an overall malaise. During that phase of my pregnancy, I wondered if my restricted movement and lack of activity was actually doing more harm than good.

I had to trust my doctor, though, and more importantly, I had to continue to trust God.

Food for Thought

Sometimes discouragement and negative thoughts take hold of us, and make us question God and the decisions we have made. Is this the right path? Am I pursuing the correct course for my life and my family? What if I harm my own health, which has been questionable in the past, in order to see this through successfully?

I dismissed those thoughts from my mind, and rejected the idea that my health would be adversely affected long term from the restrictions imposed on me during my pregnancy. I had come way, way too far to allow doubts to creep in. I found myself, once again, turning to God's word for answers to this problem. One of the best scriptures I could find on overcoming fear and doubt was **Psalm 91**.

> "I had come way, way too far to allow doubts to creep in."

Psalm 91 (NLT)

¹ Those who live in the shelter of the Most High
   will find rest in the shadow of the Almighty.
² This I declare about the Lord:
He alone is my refuge, my place of safety;
   he is my God, and I trust him.
³ For he will rescue you from every trap
   and protect you from deadly disease.
⁴ He will cover you with his feathers.

The Seventh Request

He will shelter you with his wings.
His faithful promises are your armor
and protection.
⁵ Do not be afraid of the terrors of the night,
nor the arrow that flies in the day.
⁶ Do not dread the disease that stalks
in darkness,
nor the disaster that strikes at midday.
⁷ Though a thousand fall at your side,
though ten thousand are dying around you,
these evils will not touch you.
⁸ Just open your eyes,
and see how the wicked are punished.

⁹ If you make the Lord your refuge,
if you make the Most High your shelter,
¹⁰ no evil will conquer you;
no plague will come near your home.
¹¹ For he will order his angels
to protect you wherever you go.
¹² They will hold you up with their hands
so you won't even hurt your foot on a stone.
¹³ You will trample upon lions and cobras;
you will crush fierce lions and serpents
under your feet!

¹⁴ The Lord says, "I will rescue those who
love me.
I will protect those who trust in my name.
¹⁵ When they call on me, I will answer;
I will be with them in trouble.
I will rescue and honor them.
¹⁶ I will reward them with a long life
and give them my salvation."

With each passing day, I felt God leading me closer to His complete fulfillment of my most important specific prayer request.

It was vitally important for my confidence to remain high, my thoughts to remain positive, and for me to stay focused on the goal.

13

THE SEVENTH REQUEST FULFILLED

ITEM ONE ON THE new specific prayer request sub-list, the stress level, was certainly a tough one for us to overcome, but I knew God was guiding us through it. It was a daily struggle. It seemed for weeks as though there was a new challenge or obstacle to tackle. My poor husband was under a tremendous amount of stress with his job, our pregnancy situation, and personal matters stemming from his dad, and I prayed for him to be able to handle it all without losing *his* health.

The Seventh Request

Item two on the sub-list had been covered at the end of January during the 20-week ultrasound. Thankfully, that was one worry that had been put to rest. By all appearances, she was a healthy, thriving little baby girl, and for that we were most grateful. Jacquelyn and Graham were also getting excited about the prospect of having a baby sister in the house. They were so sweet, and as helpful as a second grader and a kindergartner could be.

> *"By all appearances, she was a healthy, thriving little baby girl, and for that we were most grateful."*

The third and final item on the Seventh Request sub-list, carrying the baby to full term, was looking brighter all the time. My stress level went down a little more every time another week came off our count. I had even been formulating names in my head and running them past Don. Lying in bed one night, it came to me that I should name her Andrea, after the doctor that helped make her possible.

By week 30, I was well into the third trimester. I was feeling tremendous relief, and beginning to look forward to the big day—delivery day. I finally allowed myself to feel happy and excited about Andrea's pending arrival. Instead of praying so desperately for her to stay in, I began to relax, and really prepare for having another little person in our home.

April and May actually hummed along rather smoothly. The prenatal doctor's appointment for week 39 rolled around, and we were getting to the end of May. I was ready for Andrea to make her appearance. We all were.

> *"I was ready for Andrea to make her appearance. We all were."*

Ironically enough, after worrying and even obsessing all those months about the possibility of Andrea coming too soon, now the discussion was when to bring me in to have labor induced. During that last visit, the doctor examined me. Then she looked at me with a smile, put her hands on her hips, and said, "How do you feel about coming to the hospital to be induced tomorrow?"

Tomorrow! I felt wonderful about it! I was finally going to meet my Andrea, my Seventh Request, the person I had visualized in my mind, and prayed for with all my heart, the person I had waited over three and a half years to meet.

I felt fantastic about tomorrow.

14

THE HAPPY ENDING

I WANT TO MAKE IT clear that I do not value any one of my children more than the others. Jacquelyn and Graham's entrances into this world were no less significant to my husband and me than Andrea's. Each one has a special, unique story that stems from the days surrounding their birth. Each one was prayed for fervently, and wanted desperately. My prayer now is that each one knows how special he or she is to me, and how much their mom and dad adore them.

My older two children are adults now, married with their own lives and responsibilities. I am ecstatically thankful to have been there to see it all. They are both wonderful, and we are all very close. Andrea is a teenager—kind, compassionate, sharp as a tack (just like the others), with a cast iron will, and a true spirit of determination.

No wonder she made it so far.

The circumstances that preceded Andrea's life were unusual, and for a long time, her existence was in question. For many years, I could not bring myself to sit down and write out the events that preceded Andrea, mostly because some of them were too painful to relive. But I felt an urge, a compelling drive, to finally write down the events I have recorded in the previous chapters.

> *"Perhaps … I can inspire someone… to get through a seemingly impossible situation."*

My journey on the road to learning more about growing an effective prayer life has been particularly weighing on my mind. I know in my heart the Lord intends for me to share it with others. Perhaps in doing so, I can inspire someone, even one person, to get through a seemingly impossible situation. Perhaps by reading this story, someone else can gain comfort after experiencing a miscarriage, or an ill health diagnosis. Perhaps God wants me to teach and guide others with what I learned about how to pray specifically. I don't know what you as the reader will gain from it, but you know. And above all, God knows.

May you have His blessings and peace in your life.

NOTES

The Seventh Request

The Seventh Request

The Seventh Request

The Seventh Request

Anna Scates

The Seventh Request

The Seventh Request

The Seventh Request

Anna Scates

The Seventh Request

ABOUT THE COVER

Now that you have read through the book, I felt it was worth noting the photo on the cover is of Andrea, my Seventh Request. We shot this photo in our backyard on a very warm first day of autumn, right before dashing off to band practice.

It certainly seemed fitting to use her image to illustrate this story. I continue to thank God every day for granting my Seven Requests—in particular my Seventh—for His unfailing love and mercy, and for the blessings of my sweet husband and my three wonderful children.

About the Author

ANNA SCATES is a blogger and author. Her blog is entitled *The 7 Year Adventure—A Positive Spin on Parenting Teens*, and can be found online at 7yearadventure.com. She writes and posts articles there to guide parents of teens and to encourage them to enjoy and make the most of their kids' teen years. She has a mechanical engineering degree from Tennessee Tech University, and worked as an engineer for a few years until she decided motherhood was her greatest calling.

Anna loves pen and pencil drawing, painting, crocheting, sewing, zip-lining, and of course, writing. She lives in Franklin, Kentucky with her husband, Don, and her daughter, Andrea.

LEARN MORE AT

7YearAdventure.com

www.ingramcontent.com/pod-product-compliance
Lightning Source LLC
LaVergne TN
LVHW041338080426
835512LV00006B/520